11/15

W9-BAC-898

ZOMBIE ANIMALS
PARASITES TAKE CONTROL!

ZOMBIE ANTS

BY FRANCES NAGLE

Gareth Stevens
PUBLISHING

Please visit our website, www.garethstevens.com. For a free color catalog of all our high-quality books, call toll free 1-800-542-2595 or fax 1-877-542-2596.

Library of Congress Cataloging-in-Publication Data

Nagle, Frances.
Zombie ants / by Frances Nagle.
p. cm. — (Zombie animals: parasites take control!)
Includes index.
ISBN 978-1-4824-2828-5 (pbk.)
ISBN 978-1-4824-2829-2 (6 pack)
ISBN 978-1-4824-2830-8 (library binding)
1. Parasites — Juvenile literature. 2.Host-parasite relationships — Juvenile literature. I. Nagle, Frances. II. Title.
QL757.N36 2016
578.6—d23

First Edition

Published in 2016 by
Gareth Stevens Publishing
111 East 14th Street, Suite 349
New York, NY 10003

Designer: Nicholas Domiano
Editor: Kristen Rajczak

Photo credits: Cover, p. 1 pixelman/Shutterstock.com; pp. 5, 9 Henrik Larsson/ Shutterstock.com; p. 7 Kokhanchikov/Shutterstock.com; pp. 11, 13, 15, 17, 21 (all photos) courtesy of David P. Hughes and the team at Hughes Lab; p. 19 Michael Pettigrew/ Shutterstock.com.

Printed in the United States of America

CPSIA compliance information: Batch #CS15GS: For further information contact Gareth Stevens, New York, New York at 1-800-542-2595.

CONTENTS

Words in the glossary appear in **bold** type the first time they are used in the text.

WHAT'S WRONG WITH THE ANTS?

Have you ever seen an ant at work? It rushes along the ground, maybe carrying little pieces of food for its colony. Ants are very hardworking **insects** that don't commonly leave known trails to food and their home.

But something is taking over the brains and bodies of **tropical** carpenter ants! They walk around aimlessly, falling out of their tree **canopy** homes. Then, the ants stop and die. What's causing these ants to become zombies?

TAKE-OVER TRUTHS

CARPENTER ANTS ARE A KIND OF ANT THAT'S PART OF THE ANIMAL GROUP *CAMPONOTUS* (KAM-PUH-*NOH*-TUHS).

One **species** of carpenter ant is known for its own take-over. Black carpenter ants are known across North America for eating away at wood—sometimes inside houses' walls!

5

PARASITE PROBLEM

Zombie ants are acting strangely because they've been taken over by a parasite! A parasite is an **organism** that lives in or on another organism, called a host. The parasite benefits from this, but the host can be harmed and sometimes killed.

The parasite controlling and causing tropical carpenter ants to die is a type of **fungus** called *Ophiocordyceps* (oh-fee-oh-KOHR-dihs-ehps). There are many species of this fungus, several of which are now being studied for their ability to create zombie ants.

TAKE-OVER TRUTHS

SCIENTISTS BELIEVE ABOUT HALF OF LIFE ON EARTH IS PARASITIC. A VERY SMALL AMOUNT OF PARASITES CAN SEEM TO CONTROL THE BRAINS OF OTHER ANIMALS LIKE SPECIES OF *OPHIOCORDYCEPS*.

Many insects carry parasites that can make people sick. Mosquitoes are hosts for the tiny organisms that cause an illness called malaria.

NOT NEW NEWS

Scientists have known about zombie ants for a long time. Famous scientist Alfred Russel Wallace first observed the zombie ant fungus in 1859 in Indonesia. He found examples of it in the Amazon, too. A museum in France also had a **specimen** in the early 1900s.

Today, the carpenter ants and their fungus can be found in tropical forests, including in Thailand and Brazil. The ants live high in the canopy in nests they build in dead or wet wood.

TAKE-OVER TRUTHS

A **FOSSIL** THAT'S 48 MILLION YEARS OLD MAY SHOW SIGNS OF ZOMBIE ANTS!

Carpenter ants of many kinds live in wooded areas all over the world.

FREAKY FUNGUS

The fungus finds an ant host when ants are traveling around their forest home. The fungus's **spores** attach to an ant's hard outer covering, or exoskeleton. The fungus pushes through the exoskeleton and starts its take-over!

The fungus grows inside the ant's body, until it's filled it up. This is when the ant starts to act like a zombie! The parasite is now controlling the ant, making it walk funny and fall to lower tree branches or the forest floor.

TAKE-OVER TRUTHS

THE ANT'S BODY IS A FOOD SOURCE FOR THE FUNGUS.

Only in the past few years have scientists begun to believe that parasites could control their host.

11

THE DEATH BITE

Once the fungus has totally taken over the ant's body, the fungus sends it to a leaf just above the forest floor. Then, it has the ant bite down on the underside of the leaf. The fungus locks the ant's **jaws** so it can't fall off the leaf. The ant dies.

Within a few days, the fungus grows a stalk, or stem, that pushes through the ant's head. The stalk is what drops spores on other ants nearby, creating more zombie ants!

TAKE-OVER TRUTHS

ONLY ABOUT 6.5 PERCENT OF THE ZOMBIE ANT FUNGUS'S FRUITING BODIES—THE STALK GROWING OUT OF THE ANT'S HEAD—SUCCESSFULLY SPREAD SPORES.

This image shows what the zombie ant fungus looks like up close once it has grown through the head of the ant.

CHEMICAL CONTROL

Scientists have spent a lot of time in the past few years studying the zombie ant fungus. They've traveled to tropical forests to find places where many ants have died because of the fungus.

These studies have found that the fungus makes **chemicals** when inside the ant's body. The chemicals control the ant. However, each special species of *Ophiocordyceps* is linked to one kind of carpenter ant. The fungus only makes the special zombie chemicals when attached to its ant species!

TAKE-OVER TRUTHS

THOUGH EACH KIND OF FUNGUS CAN ONLY CONTROL ONE KIND OF CARPENTER ANT, IT CAN KILL ANY CARPENTER ANT.

The fungus tries to reach as many ants as possible by causing zombie ants to die near their colony.

ALWAYS ON TIME

The zombie ant fungus is very exact in its control of its host. The fungus makes ants go to the underside of a leaf that's facing north or northwest. The leaf is about 10 inches (25 cm) off the ground. Finally, the death bite of the ant happens right around noon, when the sun is highest in the sky.

This time and location is best for the fungus's growth. In fact, scientists tried to move dead zombie ants, and the fungus didn't grow!

TAKE-OVER TRUTHS

SCIENTISTS BELIEVE THERE COULD BE AS MANY AS 1,000 KINDS OF ZOMBIE ANT FUNGUS WE DON'T KNOW ABOUT YET!

This zombie ant has done exactly as the fungus wanted—not that it had a choice!

FIGHTING BACK

The zombie ant fungus could kill a whole ant colony—but it usually doesn't. Tropical carpenter ants have found ways of surviving. First, ants only send their oldest workers out of the nest. The young, strong ants are safe from the fungus while in the nest.

Second, ants keep their nests very clean, so any stray fungus would be removed. That includes sick ants, too! A zombie ant wouldn't be allowed to stay in the nest long enough to pass on the fungus.

TAKE-OVER TRUTHS

ANTS HAVE FOUND WAYS TO KEEP THEIR NEST SAFE TO PROTECT THE MOST IMPORTANT ANT IN THE COLONY—THE QUEEN.

THE QUEEN

Scientists think the zombie ant fungus might not be able to grow well inside ants' nests anyway.

A PARASITE'S PARASITE

Something else is stopping the zombie ant fungus from killing every carpenter ant living in the world's tropical forests. It's another parasitic fungus! This fungus stops the zombie ant fungus's fruiting bodies from making spores and taking over more ants.

The parasite that stops the zombie ant fungus actually helps the fungus in a way. It stops too many ants from dying. If too many ants die, the zombie ant fungus would have no food!

THE MAKING OF A ZOMBIE ANT

spore attaches to ant's exoskeleton and pushes through it

▼

fungus grows inside ant's body

▼

fungus makes special chemicals to control the ant

▼

ant walks away from its known trails

▼

ant bites the underside of a leaf and dies

▼

stalk grows out of the ant's head

▼

spores fall from stalk and find other ants

21

GLOSSARY

canopy: the upper branches of a forest

chemical: matter that can be mixed with other matter to cause changes

fossil: the hardened marks or remains of plants and animals that formed over thousands or millions of years

fungus: a living thing that is somewhat like a plant, but doesn't make its own food, have leaves, or have a green color. Fungi include molds and mushrooms.

insect: a small, often winged, animal with six legs and three body parts

jaws: the walls of the mouth

organism: a living thing

species: a group of plants or animals that are all the same kind

specimen: a sample of a group

spore: a small body made by a fungus that can grow into another fungus

tropical: having to do with the warm parts of Earth near the equator

FOR MORE INFORMATION

BOOKS

Ang, Karen. *Inside the Ants' Nest*. New York, NY: Bearport Publishing, 2014.

Jackson, Cari. *Bugs That Destroy*. New York, NY: Marshall Cavendish Benchmark, 2009.

WEBSITES

Ants

animals.nationalgeographic.com/animals/bugs/ant/
Learn more about all different kinds of ants, and see cool pictures.

Ants: Explore Ants

www.pestworldforkids.org/pest-guide/ants/
Some ants are considered pests, including carpenter ants. Find out more here!

INDEX